Obedience and the Holocaust

NEHEMY N. KIHARA

DEDICATION

To my late Paternal Uncle Wilson Kabiru Gathogo, who was a
World War II Veteran soldier cum Mau Mau Freedom Fighter, who
spent his youthful life as a colonial Detainee, for his
resistance to British Imperialism and oppression in Kenya.

My late paternal grandfather
Kamau[Wambugu] wa-Kihara wa-Ole' Kiniu .
World War I Veteran, who later abandoned the British as a n 'Askari'
soldier, because he could not obey their unjust laws against Africans.

To the many Jews and their supporters, who lost their life and those
that suffered more for resistance to Nazi racism and Holocaust..

Dedicated also to all those that continually refuse to
obey and comply with the laws and orders of local and global
systems of oppression and injustice

.

CONTENTS

ACKNOWLEDGMENTS

Those that participated with me in the struggle to bring
justice and democracy in Kenya.
My fellow activist clergyman and colleague Dr.Timothy Murere
Njoya of the Presbyterian Church of Eat Africa.
The late Ms.Wamere Dadet wa -Mwangi, former Head of the French
Department and fellow Activist Educator /Lecturer at Kenyatta
University, where we led many others in the struggle to bring
Academic Freedom and Excellence. ,through the
University Academic and Staff Union.
With both of these fearless Warriors we faced the KANU Regime
Appointed Public Hearings in Nyeri, ,
We voiced our opposition to the dictatorial one party and
oppressive Prez.Moi Government and gave Recommendation for
Democratic Reforms.,

1 THE PROBLEM

This paper attempts to deal with the relationship of obedience to the Holocaust. Obedience is defined in this study as the state or quality of being obedience and to the Holocaust. Obedience is defined in this study as the state or quality of being obedient and the act or practice of obeying dutifully (Random House Dictionary, 1969). Being submissive to the restraint or command of authority or submissive to the control of another. Holocaust is defined as the genocidal devastation which can result from the relationship of an oppressive authority and its human subjects.

For the purpose of this study, obedience is seen as the problem, so as to determine its role as a determinant of the behaviour of the oppressive Nazis and the oppressed Jews during the historical genocidal devastation of European Jewry by the Nazi Germany (Hitler Regime).

The study attempts to answer the following questions:

Q.1 How far was obedience a central determinant of the human capacity to commit the horror, evil and continual cruelty of genocide?

Q.2 What recalcitrant measures are there to prevent hatred and obvious genocide within the bounds of obedience to authority, especially an oppressive one?

2 BASIC ASSUMPTIONS

In this study obedience during the Holocaust is viewed as the submissive compliance with the Nazis order or authority by these officials in the Nazis administration, these followed orders, even to the extent of committing evil - genocide, while claiming to be doing their respectful duties.

On the other hand, there were those Jews who were involved in the daily tasks of running death camps by just forcefully obeying the orders of those who had imprisoned them. In these two cases, obedience or submission compliance was expected so as to keep the Holocaust processes orderly.

3 METHODOLOGY

In In this study secondary sources have been used and the data is mainly gathered through library sources.

Due to time restraint, exhaustive research of all materials especially books dealing with Holocaust was impossible, therefore a few representative books which seem to contain materials on the Holocaust and in terms of Jews obedience were used.

Mostly, the study utilizes data collected during the Hitler regime. The study stresses the emergence of patterns of obedience and recalcitrant measures by Jews through the horror of Holocaust.

4 FINDINGS:OBEDIENCE MADE THE HOLOCAUST POSSIBLE.

In my literature search on the relationship of obedience to Holocaust, two differing views emerge. One is represented by Brune Bettelheim (Bettelheim, 1979) while the other is represented by Torrance De Pres (de Pres, 1979).

In his writings, Bettelheim develops the psychoanalytic theory that says that "in extreme situations the majority of adult human beings will regress to childlike behavior, accepting the values and intentions of their assailants (and go to their death like lemmings) or follow their death tendencies even to suicide". Yet he qualifies this through an emphasis of the fact that through the Holocaust the Jewish people survived.

In regard to the central argument of this study, Bettelheim represents the view that takes Jewish passivity for granted in the face of the impeding disaster, especially when he attempts to show adult prisoners falling into anonymous mass and behaving like incompetent children (Bettelheim, 1960).

This was probably done to explain why some Jewish prisoners survived through their involvement in the running of the camps of death ... starvation, beatings, sickness, exhaustion and random death. They had lived in this world of filth, pain and constant danger by doing the work detail and involvement in the genocide process in gas chambers made for them by the Nazis.

In contrast, de Press tells another side that takes for granted that Jews' (human beings') will to resist. This reality was manifested in the eventual revolt of the prisoners and the destruction of the death camps especially Treblinka (De Pres, 1979) where the Jews rose up and fought the Nazis against all odds, hoping that at least one among them could survive to tell the world of their survival not through obedience but through recalcitrant measures.

While both Bettelheim and De Pres are considered as spokesmen for the Holocaust survival and survivors, one should not think of either being ignorant of the two sides of the dilemma in question, yet on the basis of their writings they differ in the degree of what each emphasized in the Holocaust situations and events.

On the basis of their writings we can tentatively conclude that Bettelheim emphasize (not justifies) the Jewish obedience as a means of survival, while De Pres seems to emphasize the recalcitrant measures or the Jewish will to resist as a means of survival.

Other literature considered on Holocaust (Frankel), emphasize the human capacity to commit evil and potential for radical madness. However he fails to give us any answers to the questions posed.

Hanna Arendt 19 brings yet another dimension of our observation that is the question of those in the Nazi regime who were involved in evil (as a matter of duty) in the regime who were involved in evil (as a matter of duty) in the regime who were involved in evil (as a matter of duty) in the second Reich and its Nazi Policies.

The question here is how for the German population as a whole participated or partook in the murder of Euro-Jews and to what extent we justify or blame them?

Last but also important, is the study by Milgram, (Milgram, 1974). Obedience experiments which shows us the nature of human obedience to authority and how far it can go. Milgram conducted an experiment where by human beings were to obey inorder to resist electric shock.

While 2/3 of those experimented on obeyed without question, 1/3 resulted to recalcitrant measures and resisted the orders despite the consequences of high voltage of electric shock, (Baver, 1979) emphasized Jews resistance during the Holocaust.

The literature mentioned was reviewed on the basis of their discussion of the role of obedience in the Holocaust situation and finally some possible measures to prevent the occurrence of genocide or another Holocaust are suggested.

In the final analysis recalcitrant measures as the resistance to hatred and oppression will be mentioned for further study. The significance of this study lies in its attempt to show that it is the human minds that evil and hatred is created which leads to genocide or possible Holocaust, and it is their minds that we should study so as to alter their prejudices before prevention can be made possible.

If by obeying the Hitler Regime, the German masses partook in the Holocaust evil, then by recalcitrant measures some opposed his policies and indeed took away the blame from German masses. On the other side, if by being passive the Jews were also used to their own destruction, then through recalcitrant measures, some resisted and survived. Therefore, there is hope that such a planned mass murder can be fought back and stopped (Dawidowiez 1975).

5 NAZI DUTIFUL COMPLIANCE

If there were one thing that the Nazis can be better categorized with, it is their attention to order and efficiency.

During Holocaust which was characterized with bloodshed and madness, Nazis higher officials were not directly involved in the day-to-day craziness but they oversaw the whole operation, while others did their daily routine which was well organized and established by Hitler's regime.

The Holocaust started because of the hatred of Hews. The fore runners of Hitler's Antisemitism had advocated the forcible extirpation of the Jews as early as the beginning of the last century (Friedman, 1954).

The demand was repeated several times in the course of the latter part of the century and the early twentieth century. Hitler himself demanded the removal of the Jews as early as 1919. Jews had been made scapegoats in the German discussions of the falling economy.

The destruction of Euro-Jews as De Pres states (De Pres, 1979) had no rational reason or motive, nor plunder, politics, military strategy or blind expediency could justify its existence.

However the absolute death of all Jews in Europe became a Hitler's decree and Nazi camps were established in 1933 as soon as he came to power. These camps were also meant to be training places of S.S. (Gestapo) and detention centers. After the outbreak of the war these centers became the extermination centers of Euro-Jews.

The Nazi policy was a prejudiced one based on racism and a system of cover-up. Their racism was based on two blood types. That of blood purity or good blood and bad one.

The term "blood was used as a transmitter of inherent moral and cultural as well as physical qualities. Good blood was Germanic blood based on the purity of white (Aryan) race. This was a rationalization of hatred of Jews.

Thus camps were established outside Reich so that Germany could commit genocide without training their soil which made them think in their minds that they were pure. A few of the camps includes Auschwitz, Brikenau, Maudenk, Chelmao, Belzec and Sobibor which were named for rural villages of Eastern Europe. Auschwitz served as the administrative center for other camp systems.

These camps were geographically remote but were connected by massive system of railway that shipped human cargo marked "special treatment".

Therefore Hitler's vast power ran wild, and the evil of the final solution to the Jewish question was established in system of functioning structures and could be no longer be stopped by the counter forces within it.

Those in service to their beloved land, found the state so powerful and the evil deployment greater than their will. No matter how irrational they found the Nazi policy to be, what else could they do but to do their duty or paperwork (Flershner, 1977)? This dutiful compliance is what can be categorized here as the German role of obedience during Holocaust.

For German's, their lives were lived in their gigantic undertakings of their modernized factory systems which produced glorified war machines and final product of death. Yet this daily routine of just "doing their work" made them so blind to the realities of life and human dignity.

Obedience on the case of Germans was based on the premises that were nurtured by Christianity, "Obey those that are in authority for they are God's servants over you (Romans 13;3)".

But how could Hitler be God's servants? At the same time, being so powerful a leader who could say that he was not? Some conscious Germans did say that he was demonic and as a result they were imprisoned or detained. Their recalcitrant measures teach us that there is strength of human decency and goodness in resistance.

6 JEWISH SUBMISSIVE COMPLIANCE

Bruno Bettelheim was one of the major spokesman of the Jews survivors. In his book (Bettelheim, 1966) he remarks "walking to the gas chamber was committing suicide in a way that asked for none of the energy usually needed in deciding to kill oneself".

Psychologically speaking, most prisoners in the extermination camps committed suicide by submitting to death without resistance (De Pres, 1979). As mentioned elsewhere Bettelheim suggests that Jews' submissive compliance to the orders in the Nazi camps amounted to obedience.

However, there are other accounts and explanations that see this differently. Jews were baffled and their escape from the Ghettos or the death camps was suppressed because their resistance would have endangered their whole family.

They also felt that they were not to be killed, that they were too valuable, and that the Germans needed their labor, their talents, and even their money. **Many believed that if they obeyed the law, they would be spared.** Orthodox Jews refused to resist militarily because to them resistance was disobedience to God's law, which was considered suicide. They therefore had hope of survival.

The other belief on why Jews complied was that they did not have arms and there was lack of trust. lack of communication between Jews and their outside world and trained leadership contributed to their obedience. This problem was sometimes due to anti-Semitism or fear of Germans.

Therefore it is feasible to believe that Jews complied because of the incomprehensibility of the Holocaust itself, principles of collective responsibility, lack of arms and trust and hope of survival.

In some instances the Jews resisted through armed rebellion. Some examples of such rebellions include the Warsaw Ghetto rebellion which evolved in April 1943. Other Ghetto resistances through rebelling includes the Bialystok, the Vilna and many more.

These revolts through recalcitrant measures had some heroes who survived to tell and testify that even in the most odd situations, life can triumph over its governing death. Human potential for radical evil can be controlled.

7 CRUELTY AND GENOCIDE FUELED BY OBEDIENCE

As we have observed, the role played by submissive obedience by the Nazi officials produced the sort of cruelty and oppressions that could only in the final stages result into genocide.

Hitler's "plan of the Master Race" was to build a people, `folk' whose superiority could only be achieved by bloodshed.

In other words the Master Race could only be produced by the German folks being conquerors, that is militarily subduing all those in their vicinity especially in Eastern Europe (Moore, 1978).

So as to present a practical ideology, the image of the Aryan descendants had to be brought to the focus. And this required that the undesirables like the Gypsies and the Jews (who were in different national boundaries) be made the scapegoat or the racial problem that needed a solution.

After his rather successful conquest of Eastern European nations surrounding him and the outbreak of what was later to be known as the World War II, his power ran wild and the final solution was found in the complete extermination of the Euro-Jews.

What still remains a dilemma to us is the fact that the German masses and the officials in particular by their mere dutiful submission, spent much of their energies in the modernized war factories producing weapons of cruelty and oppression.

There was no doubt in Nazi Germany, that the dictator Hitler, spoke of the power of symbolic manipulation and he was ill deadly earnest when he argued that only through idealism, could a nation willingly spill the blood required to reach higher ends.

However this marvels us, that when his demonic power picked its momentum the more evil it became, but thanks to recalcitrant human measures.

Despite the fact that, obedience played a central role in the Holocaust events, measures of recalcitrant action were potential among the Jews and some conscious Germans. On this basis, the German masses cannot as a people be held responsible for a bureaucracy run wild.

Although partly, they may admit a certain amount of responsibility of obedience to the Nazi Regime in its development to a World Enemy 'numeral one'.

On the side of the Jews who were rounded up to the death camps despite of lack of appropriate words to explain how they submitted to authority, in most cases without resistance, we can still today say as De Pres claimed that the "will of some to do evil in our human structures, there exists an old heroic ethic, wherein the individual, as an individual, defies power and willingly dies for a glorious cause".

What **the recalcitrant measures** of the Jews at Treblinka taught us is that, we need to redefine our theology and philosophy that considers obedience and duty, despite the right and justice that should be their base.

8 RECALCITRANCE: RESISTANCE TO OPPRESSION AND GENOCIDE

One of the lessons that De Pres has been trying to teach is the fact that the hopelessness that can be seen in the Jewish Holocaust is counterbalanced by the fact that the Jews rather than being passive and childish puppets of an oppressive situation emerged as heroes.

Treblinka is a case that redefined heroism in the dilemma of the Jewish Holocaust. As the largest camp of all the other five, which included Auschwitz, records were kept of the numbers of prisoners coming in and the genocide process which was well planned.

Each day 20,000 human beings were turned from flesh to smoke, a literal Holocaust, a complete extermination of human beings into nil. Yet on August 2, 1943,600 victims staged a revolt.

These became obstinately defiant of authority ,which means that that they stubbornly disobeyed. Stubbornly disobeyed, because they were well aware of the punishment to such a behavior that moves out of the ordinary order, which was submissive obedience to the camp roles and authority.

As a result of their revolt, almost all of them died, but to celebrate a new chapter of human heroism, 40 of them survived. The eventual revolt of these human beings, the total destruction of the camp and the fact that they fought to death for life and its dignity is the fact that this study celebrates.

Many of the Jews did not know that by not resisting the Nazi in recalcitrant manner, they were going to their own death. By this passivity they had implicated themselves to their own death, (Steiner, 1966).

Of course, one realizes that to make such an analogy seems ridiculous, in the face of the horror of the Holocaust, but this simply means that this stage of our study of the relationship of "Obedience and the Holocaust" ; we cannot simply blame the masses of either Germans or the European Jews, without implicating the other.

In the close examination of the role played by the Germans and the Jews, as far as `obedience' is concerned, the Holocaust seems to lead us to a "mockery situation" where as human beings, we are ashamed of what the dilemma teaches us.

One, the fact that a lot of Germans claimed only to be doing their job, despite the evil that this way of "earning a living" produced, makes us think our own call of duty and the possibility of evil it can produce.

As Milgram's obedience study revealed, our own commitment and obedience to authority in the form of modern bureaucracies, needs to be examined, so as to determine how far we are willing to go.

To put this in a question form, does our own "call of duty" allow enough room for recalcitrant measures when the bureaucracy seems to be treading on an evil path?

9 CONCLUSION

In our globe today the Holocaust situations are imminent. In the history of European colonialism and imperialism a lot of genocide was committed to the masses of people, today inhabiting the third world. Wars never known to most of them, apart from a few ethnic frictions, became a reality in Africa, Asia and Latin America, and the situation still continues.

Oppressive regimes - either of the left or of the right have come and gone and some are still continuing, almost all of them at one state or the other have enjoyed Western support -- Chile, Nicaragua, Uganda, Chad, Cambodia, Iran, Central African, Republic, Equatorial Guinea, Zaire, Burundi, Haiti and Vietnam and South Korea and elsewhere, I dare to mention.

The list is longer according to the records on the abuse of human rights, monitored by Amnesty International.

In 1980s, the South Africa white minority regime, supported by less than 4 million light skinned Euro-descendants, abuses daily the human rights of over 20 million African peoples with its Nazi inspired apartheid system.

Worse, they claim to be based in Christian principles and civilization, which had produced the ideology of separate but unequal development of the races with the Master "white" race at the top of the ladder.

Reports after reports have been filed about this demonic regime, whose cruel treatment of African masses has become so deliberate, that they have become so blind to see the reality of an obvious armed resistance.

Certain similarities can be drawn between the Nazi Regime and the South African Boer "white" minority regime; even if we decide not to mention their historic relationship many years ago and the immigration of Nazi criminals who found refuge there after the fall of Hitler.

Of course, the particularity of the Holocaust is the show case of the human capacity to commit evil and terror, and the capacity to target, isolate and ultimately destroy those within society who have become "superfluous persons" as put by Rubenstein (1975).

An itemization of the genocide committed during the Holocaust seems to us so demonic, therefore the records continue with no summed up meaning. It is so terrifying, sickening and shameful that 11 million people were exterminated in five years, at least 6 million of them Jews, 2 million of them children, who were dumped into living ditches of framed and crazy medical experiments.

The Auschwitz events still haunt us so deeply that we are ashamed of our own capacity to commit evil. And yet we seem to be blind in this Western culture to be ready to go to war on an Indochinese nation allied to the Eastern Block when it quarrels with its sister Indochinese nation allied to their ideology.

At the same time they ignorde a demonic white minority regime, even Israel had some dealings with them., even when its politico-economic institutions had internationally been recognized even by the United Nations to be against Human Rights.

The Southern African case was another Nazi type of situation, the minority regime in the name of a few white Afrikaners had created a situation of a total death camps for the Africans in their own land. In the name of Western democracy and Christian civilization they had developed a demonic capacity where they had warfare industries capable of making an atomic bomb.

Because the leadership is "white" the so called 'white' Western European nations and their allies (almost all of them former colonizers) still did not for a long time consider, the South African regime a serious threat to human life and dignity. Instead of taking strong joint active to stop a possible Holocaust, they continue a mere lip service to the U.N. Embargo resolutions.

It is the Author's wish to mention South Africa here because it provides a good case of a modern day state build on similar principles like the Nazi, which contains the seeds of genocide and to many observations by other scholars involved in the preservation of human dignity and justice, one of the most serious "Holocaust potential situations" in the 1990s.

Other isolated situations have been mentioned, especially those of Indo-Chinese, communist regimes and explosive Middle East, South American and African nations.

The Holocaust even teaches us that there are certain issues central in the Western culture and Christian thought that need to be observed.

1. The hypocritical relationship between the Christian as the Christ lover and the Jew - the crucified Jesus and the Pharisees - the Jewish killers of Christ. This needs to be reformulated and changed so as not to be used further in fueling unnecessary animosity.

2. The legislation enacted against the Jews by the Church from Synod of Elvira in 306 to the Council of Basel in 1434 was duplicated point for point by the Nazis and used their anti-Jewish propaganda.

3. Martin Luther's frightful incitement to violence and pillage in a letter written against the Jews and their lies was also another document used for Nazis' purposes.

4. Also we need to guide a near identification of the gospel with regiment civil religion, and with a peculiarly German version of the secular, which permitted the willing seduction of a large number of the rational faithful from their legitimate calling.

With this observation we can say that what Camus (1974) called the "Administrative Murder" (wherein human beings are regarded as objects to be clearly and neatly disposed of by way of a few freight trains by a few engineers and few chemists) can no longer just happen without recalcitrant measures being taken.

In our age of totalitarian government and mass murder, the Holocaust reminds us of the genocidal situations that our hatred can produce. At the same time it teaches us and gives us hope and human dignity, to know that some people, no matter how few are willing to organize themselves in resistance to oppression and hatred so as to restore back our humanness.

The ethnic animosity in Burundi and Rwanda, where you have Hutu majority in both nations and the minority Tutsi always in hatred and tension.

The Belgian and French colonizers, had created a so called 'tribal differentiation and identification in which the Tutsi were supposed to be preferable over the Hutu. In colonial privileged arrangements these belonged to different stocks of 'tribal' classification.

Hutu could not be trusted with any leadership or responsibility in security .Tutsi made good military an d policing officers. They were also supposed to be good administrators o the colonial law and order.

There were also superimposed interpretations of assumed 'tribal' subsistence in which Hutu were plant cultivators and Tutsi were pastoral and animal keepers.

These are related people, who have always intermarried and speak the same languages, even before the dawn of European colonialism. The so called 'tribal animosity' is a creation of colonial domination, and have nothing to do with heritage or traditions.

However in Rwanda with 100 hundred days, more than 800,000 Tutsi and their Hutu supporters, died at the hands of angry Hutu. The main cause was social arrangement prejudice and politico-economic privileges that emerged from colonialism and existed during independence.

It is shameful that when the killings were going on, the western world ,just watched and took measures to stop the genocide at a very late stage.

Further Study

1. The relationship between obedience and the Holocaust needs further study probably utilizing social psychology and philosophy so that an examination of the Judeo-Christian tradition and western culture may be done.

2. The measure that would prevent hatred and genocide explored so that ills like racism can be combated and completely eradicated.

3. The Christian-Jewish relationship should be further exploded so as to safeguard illustrations of their seemingly false and hostile relationships well characterized by the historical events climaxed by the Holocaust.

10 REFERENCES

Bauer, Yehuda (1979). The Jews Emergency from Powerlessness. Toronto University of Toronto Press.

Bettelheim, Bruno (1979). The Survival and other Essays.
New York: Alfred A. Knof. The Informed Heart. Glencoe, Illinois: Free Press.

_____ (1960). The Informed Heart.

Camus, Albert (1974). Resistance, Rebellion and Death.
New York: Vintage Books.

Dawodpwcz, Lucy (1975). The War Against the Jews.
New York: Holt, Rinehart, Winston.

De Pres, Terrence ( ). The Survival: An anatomy of Life
and Death Camps.

Fein, Helen (1979). Accounting for Genocide. National Responses and Jews Victimization during Holocaust. New York: The Free Press.

Flershner, Eva (1977). Auschwitz, the Beginning of a New Era.

New York: KTVA.

Franklin, Watta. A History of the Holocaust.

Friendman, Philips (1954). Martyrs and Fighters.
New York: Crown.

GarlinskiI, Joseph (1975). Fighting Auschwitz. New York:
Harper and Row.

Hilberg, Raul (1961). The Destruction of European Jewry-
1933-1945. Chicago: Quadrangle Books.

Issac, Jules (1964). The Teaching of Contempt: Christian Roots of
Anti-Semitism Trans. Helen Weaver, New York: Holt, Rinehart, and
Winston.

Milgram, Stanley (1974).   Obedience to Authority: An
Experimental View. New York: Harper and Row.

Moore, Barrinston (1978).   Injustice: The Social Base of
Obedience and Revolt. White Plains: Sharp.

Porter, I.M. (ed.) (1974). Martin Luther: Selected Political
Writings. New York: Fortress, 1974.

Reitlinger, Gerald (1961). The Final Solution: The Attempt to
Exterminate the Jews of Europe 1933-1945 (2nd rev.) and enlarged
ed. South Brunswick, N.J.: Yoseloff.

Rubenstein, Richard (1975). The Cunning of History;
New York: Harper and Row.

Steinberg, Lucien (1974). Not as a Lamb. The Jews Against
Hitler. Tran. Marion Hunter. Farasborough, England: Saxon House.

Steiner, Jean Francois (1966). Treblinka. France.

Weber, Max (1930). The Protestant Ethic and the Spirit of Capitalism. Tran. Talcott Parsons. New York: Scribner's.

Witney, Stephens, B. (1962). "Reaction to Uncertain Threat". In Man and Society in Disaster. Ed. George W. Baker and Dwight W. Chapman. New York: Basic Books, 1962.

Wolfenstein, Martha (1957). Disaster: A Psychological Essay. New York: The Free Press and Falcon's Wing Press, 1957.

Zahn, Gordon (1962). German Catholics and the Hitler's Wars: A Study in Social Control. New York: Shed and Ward

ABOUT THE AUTHOR

The Revd. Prof. Dr. Nehemy Ndirangu Kihara was born in Nanyuki in Laikipia County of Kenya, East Africa.

He was educated at Timau in Meru County and Nairobi before graduating with a Licentiate of Theological Education from St. Paul's University (United Theological College), Limuru in Kiambu County.

He holds a Bachelor of Theology (B.Th.) in Biblical Literature and Geographic History from Christian International College.

He graduated and attained with honors a Master of Divinity (M.Div.) in Social Ethics, Psychology of Religion and Counseling, from the Interdenominational Theological Center at the Clark Atlanta University Complex.

He also attained a Doctor of Philosophy (Ph.D.) in Anthropology, Sociology of Religion and Political Science from Emory University.

As an Investigative Journalist and Radio Broadcaster this Independent Publisher hosted a weekend English and still hosts a weekly Swahili Community Show for Sagal Radio Services at WATB 1420 AM Station in Decatur, GA.

As an Interdisplinary Educator he taught Security Management and Police Studies for the Institute of Peace and Security Studies, (now known as the Department of Security and Correctional Science) of Kenyatta University in Nanyuki Campus, where he was the Coordinator of Humanities and Examinations Officer.

The Author also taught Introductory Psychology, Sociology, Criminal Procedure and Law of Evidence, Intelligence-Led Policing, Public Administration and General Management Principles among other units at the Nyeri and Embu Campuses.

He was an Adjunct Professor of Sociology/ Social Sciences at the Atlanta Campus of Saint Leo University, Tampa, Fl. Taught such courses as Anthropology, Sociology, and Criminal Justice units as Social Theory, Drugs and Society, Marriage and Family, Research Methods, Human Behavior, among others He was an Adjunct Professor of Ethics at the Georgia Campus (Henry Medical Center) of the College of Health, University of St. Francis, Joliet, Ill.,

The Author was also the founding Moderating Bishop of the Ujamaa Nomadic Church -Without Borders, as a new church- mission initiative in US. He had also been an Urban Renewal/ Organizing Pastor of Beth Salem United Presbyterian Church, Columbus, Georgia. He served as an International Missionary in California, Iowa and New York, under the Mission to US program of the Presbyterian Church, USA.

As a Senior Lecturer at Kenyatta University, the Author taught African Culture, Belief Systems, Social Theory and Research Methods units in the Department of Philosophy and Religious Studies and also in the Department of Sociology.

He was also an Activist Educator, who fought for academic freedom and excellence, which led to his unfair dismissal by the government which controlled the public universities and educational institutions. Reverend Professor Ndirangu Kihara started his career a high school teacher and principal at Muthithi Secondary School, and then an ordained Church Minister of Muthithi Parish and the Stated Clerk of the wider Murang'a Presbytery of the Presbyterian Church of East Africa.

BLUERGREEN PUBLISHING